PARIS

- **A** ABBESSES
- **B** BASTILLE
- **É** CHAMPS-ÉLYSÉES
- **F** FOLIES BERGÈRE
- **G** GALERIES LAFAYETTE
- **H** HÔTEL DE VILLE
- **Î** ÎLE SAINT-LOUIS
- **J** JARDIN DU LUXEMBOURG
- **L** LOUVRE
- **N** NOTRE-DAME
- **O** OPÉRA
- **P** CENTRE POMPIDOU
- **Q** QUARTIER LATIN
- **R** ROLAND GARROS
- **S** SACRÉ-COEUR
- **T** TOUR EIFFEL
- **U** UNESCO
- **X** XÈME ARRONDISSEMENT
- **Z** ZOO DE VINCENNES

17e

16e

8e

7e

15e

Paris is divided into twenty administrative districts called arrondissements. Numbered from 1 to 20, they spiral out from the center of the city. The *e* after 1e, 2e, 3e, 4e, etc. is the French equivalent to the English 1st, 2nd, 3rd, 4th, etc.

For Aurorus Dinosaurus

Published by Sourcebooks Jabberwocky, an imprint of Sourcebooks, Inc.
P.O. Box 4410, Naperville, Illinois 60567-4410
(630) 961-3900
Fax: (630) 961-2168
sourcebooks.com

Originally published in 2018 in Great Britain by Hodder Children's Books, an imprint of Hodder and Stoughton.

Library of Congress Cataloging-in-Publication Data is on file with the publisher.

Source of Production: Shenzhen Wing King Tong Paper Products Co. Ltd., Shenzhen, Guangdong Province, China
Date of Production: July 2018
Run Number: 5012131

Printed and bound in China.
WKT 10 9 8 7 6 5 4 3 2 1

P IS FOR PARIS

PAUL THURLBY

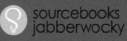
sourcebooks
jabberwocky

ABBESSES

Abbesses is the area of Montmartre where the film *Amélie*, starring Audrey Tautou, was set. With its cobbled streets, bakeries, and many pavement cafés, it is quintessential Paris.

The Art Nouveau awning at the Métro station is one of only a few original glass-covered entrances designed by Hector Guimard still present in Paris.

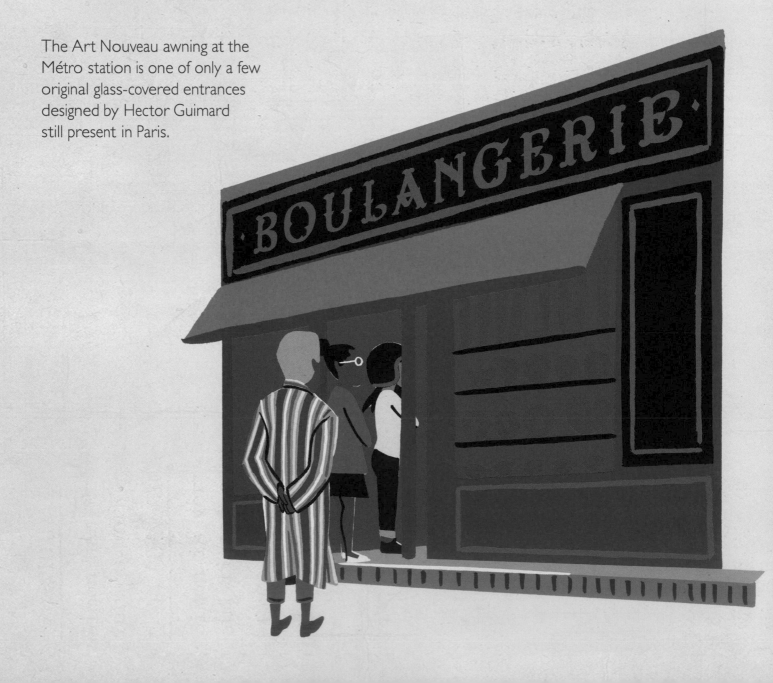

The Place de la Bastille was the site of a prison until 1790. The Storming of the Bastille on July 14, 1789 (now Bastille Day) was one of the most dramatic moments of the French Revolution. Demonstrations often take place here now.

Most of the prisoners kept in the Bastille prison were enemies of the monarch, Louis XVI. Famous inmates included the writer Voltaire, the politician Nicolas Fouquet, and the Marquis de Sade.

BASTILLE

Paris's many cafés are the perfect place to sit outside and indulge in the most Parisian of activities: people-watching!

One of Paris's most renowned cafés is the Café de Flore, located in the heart of Saint-Germain. Its famous clientele has included Picasso, Brigitte Bardot, Ernest Hemingway, and Yves Saint Laurent.

LE CAFÉ

ELACROIX

Eugène Delacroix was a French Romantic artist best known
for his famous painting *Liberty Leading the People*, exhibited
in the Louvre. Created in 1830, it celebrates the revolutionary
spirit of the French people.

EUGÈNE
DELACROIX

VINCENT
VAN GOGH

HENRI
MATISSE

PAUL
CÉZANNE

CLAUDE
MONET

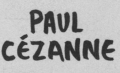

Delacroix was a major influence on some of the world's most famous artists, including Matisse, Van Gogh, Monet, Gauguin, and Cézanne.

DELACROIX

CHAMPS-ÉLYSÉES

The Avenue des Champs-Élysées is one of the most famous boulevards in the world. At 1.2 miles long and 230 feet wide, it stretches from the Place de la Concorde to the Place Charles de Gaulle, site of the Arc de Triomphe.

The Grand Palais sits at the end of the Champs-Élysées and is used for exhibitions, although during World War II, the Nazis used it to store their tanks.

FOLIES BERGÈRE

The Folies Bergère is a legendary music hall and variety-entertainment theater that opened in 1869. It has showcased the talents of many of the greatest French entertainers, such as Mistinguett, Maurice Chevalier, and Josephine Baker.

American-born Josephine Baker lit up Paris in the 1920s with her uninhibited dancing. She was given a medal for her work with the French Resistance after World War II.

GALERIES LAFAYETTE

Galeries Lafayette is a famous upmarket
department store that opened in 1912.
It has hosted international celebrities including
the Duchess of Windsor, Bill Clinton, and Prince Charles.

The dome rises to a height of 141 feet
and has become an iconic symbol of the
Galeries Lafayette.

GALERIES LAFAYETTE

HÔTEL DE VILLE

The Hôtel de Ville (city hall) is one of the most enduring landmarks of the city. It is the official office of the Mayor of Paris.

In 1792, a guillotine was installed on Place de Grève in front of the Hôtel de Ville. Crowds would gather to watch the gory spectacle. But, don't worry, the last execution took place in 1830.

ÎLE SAINT-LOUIS

The Île Saint-Louis is one of two natural islands on the River Seine in the center of Paris. While much of Paris has been modernized over the years, this enchanting isle remains frozen in the seventeeth century. It's a must on any romantic's itinerary.

The île is famous for Berthillon's ice cream.
Lines outside the famous shop regularly
stretch all the way down the street.

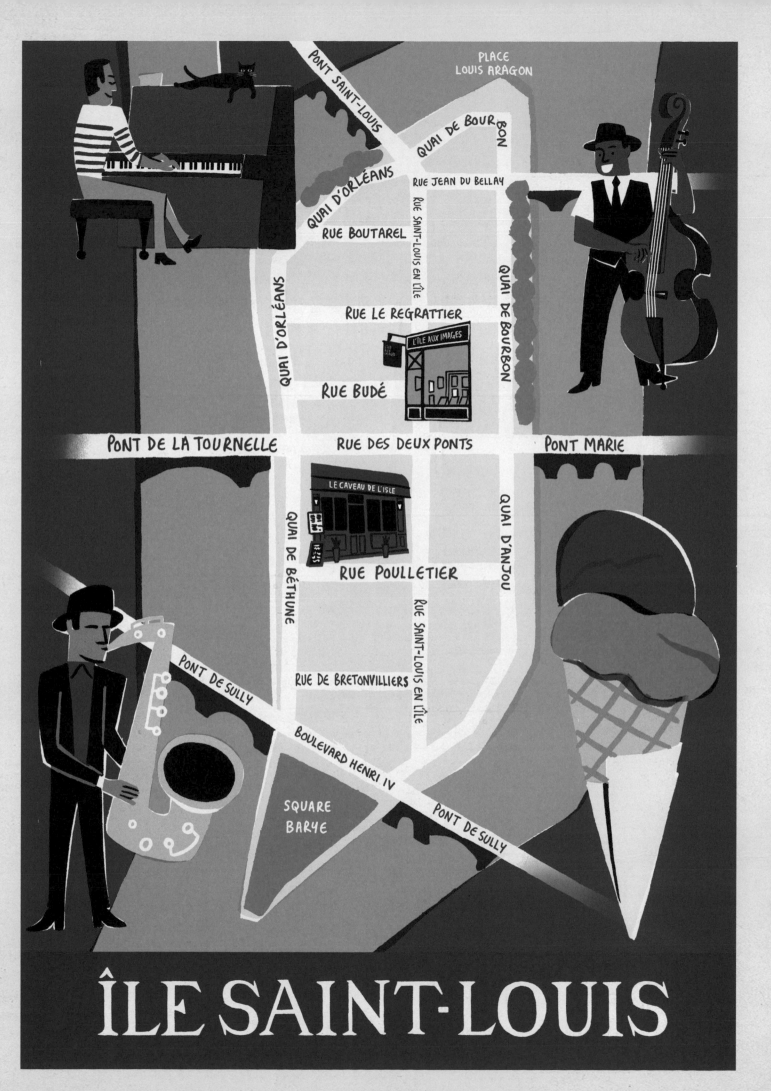

ÎLE SAINT-LOUIS

The Jardin du Luxembourg is a former royal park in the heart of Paris that features both French and English gardens, hundreds of statues, and many activities for kids.

Covering over 61 acres, this is the second largest park in Paris.

JARDIN DU LUXEMBOURG

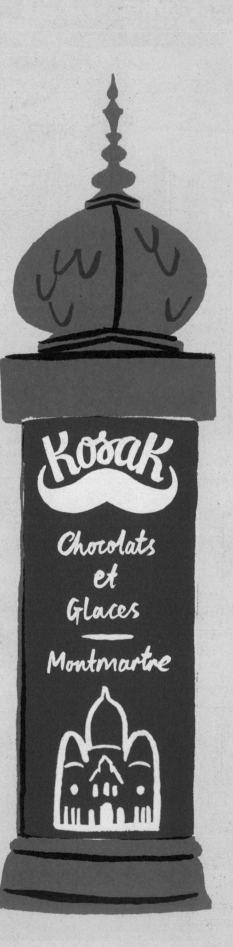

KIOSQUE

These dark-green octagonal kiosques, selling newspapers and magazines, are a familiar sight on the streets of Paris. There are hundreds of them in the city, dating back as far as 1857.

These elegant green columns, known as colonnes Morris (Morris columns) are used to advertise movies, plays, concerts, and many other attractions.

LOUVRE

The Louvre is the world's BIGGEST museum! It welcomes over 20,000 visitors a day. Entrance is via a striking glass pyramid.

The *Mona Lisa* is one of the most famous pieces of art in the world. Painted by Leonardo da Vinci, it has its own security guards and is protected by bulletproof glass.

After viewing the *Mona Lisa*, find some of the other artworks of note on display.

The Paris Métro is one of the busiest subway systems in Europe, and one of the densest in the world. Châtelet-Les Halles is the world's largest underground station.

The Paris Métro, short for Le Métropolitain, is a rapid transit system under the city of Paris. Its 300 stations are known for their distinct art nouveau style of architecture.

NOTRE-DAME

Notre-Dame cathedral is located on the Île de la Cité. It's famous for its Gothic architecture and as the setting of French novelist Victor Hugo's 1831 book *The Hunchback of Notre-Dame*.

Browsing the iconic green stalls of the bouquinistes, or riverside booksellers, along the banks of the Seine is a quintessentially Parisian pastime.

OPÉRA

Built from 1861 to 1875, Palais Garnier is one of the most famous opera houses in the world. Its sumptuous design, particularly the magnificent double staircase leading to the grand foyer, is reminiscent of the opulent Palace of Versailles.

The basement of the Palais Garnier flooded when the building was first built, inspiring the legend of an underground lake featured in the book and musical, *The Phantom of the Opera*.

POMPIDOU PIPES

Known locally as the "Beaubourg," the Centre Pompidou is a multicultural complex with the largest modern art museum in Europe. It contains over 100,000 works.

All the plumbing, electrical wiring, air circulation ducts, and even the escalators are on the outside, giving the building its unique appearance.

CENTRE POMPIDOU

QUARTIER LATIN

The Quartier Latin is found on the left bank of the River Seine. The area is associated with artists, intellectuals, and a bohemian way of life.

A favorite stop is the Shakespeare and Company bookshop near Notre-Dame.

The area got its name from the many students who studied Latin at the famous Sorbonne University.

ROLAND GARROS

The French Open, also called Roland Garros, is the only Grand Slam tennis tournament played on clay. Rafael "King of Clay" Nadal has won the championship a record eleven times!

The iconic red clay was first used in 1880 in Cannes, where powdered terra-cotta was used to cover grass courts that were wilting in the heat.

ROLAND GARROS

Sacré-Coeur

Sacré-Coeur Basilica is, for many visitors, the classic image of romantic Paris. Parisians, however, call it "the giant meringue." If you walk up to the very top of the building, you can enjoy breathtaking views of the city.

Construction began in 1875 and was completed in 1914. The cathedral is located at the summit of the Butte Montmartre, the highest point in Paris.

The Eiffel Tower (known in French as the Tour Eiffel) is one of the most iconic landmarks in the world. It was designed by Gustave Eiffel and completed on March 31, 1889. Standing 1,063 feet tall and weighing 10,100 tons, the tower was the world's tallest man-made structure for forty-one years.

In 1944, as the Allies approached Nazi-occupied Paris, Hitler ordered Dietrich von Choltitz, the city's German military governor, to demolish the tower, along with other famous monuments, including Notre-Dame. Luckily, Choltitz refused.

TOUR EIFFEL

UNESCO's goal of international cooperation to increase
universal respect through education has never been more important.

UNESCO, the United Nations Educational, Scientific and Cultural Organization, was formed on November 16, 1945. From its headquarters in Paris, UNESCO promotes peace through literacy, cultural diversity, freedom of the press, and many other educational aims.

UNESCO

VÉLIB'

Vélib', combining the words vélo (bike) and liberté (freedom), is a large-scale public bicycle sharing system in Paris.

Both mechanical and electric bikes are available.

The picturesque towns of Fontainebleau, Provins, and Moret-sur-Loing are among the favorite out-of-town destinations for Parisian families.

Whether it's spent enjoying the culture, shops, cafés, and restaurants of the city, or traveling out of town to the countryside or beach, le weekend (or la fin de semaine) is sacred to all Parisians!

The Xème (tenth) arrondissement is one of the twenty administrative districts of Paris and centers on the Canal Saint-Martin. It is home to the historic Place de la République.

The Xème contains two of the main train stations in Paris: Gare du Nord and Gare de l'Est.

XÈME ARRONDISSEMENT

YVES SAINT LAURENT

French fashion designer Yves Saint Laurent is famous for reinventing menswear for women. An icon of female empowerment, his creations include the women's trench coat, tuxedo pantsuit, and jumpsuit.

Yves Saint Laurent became Christian Dior's design assistant at the age of nineteen, and took over the couture house after Dior's death in 1957. After Saint Laurent's debut collection with Dior, French newspapers reported that he had "saved France."

YVES SAINT LAURENT

The Parc Zoologique de Paris is found in the Bois de Vincennes, Paris's largest public park. It is divided into five geographical zones where animals live in their native environment: Sahel-Sudan, Patagonia, Europe, Amazon-Guyana, and Madagascar.

The iconic Grand Rocher, a 213-foot fake boulder, has become the symbol of the zoo.

When I started working on these city books, Paris was at the very top of my list. It has a special place in my heart after a visit in 2012 when I met some locals of Montmartre who are now very good friends of mine. I've included famous landmarks and streets, but there are many other amazing places in Paris too.

The first illustration

that I draw is always the most important because it sets the tone for the rest of the book. I picked Sacré-Coeur to begin with as it's one of the most iconic buildings in Paris. Originally, I was reluctant to focus too much on the actual building because of the Parisians' dislike of it. So, I added views of the Parisian rooftops in front of it, but it still didn't look quite right.

I worked a lot on screen to try and get the composition balanced. At one stage, I wanted to include the famous steps leading up to Sacré-Coeur but it was looking a bit too overcrowded.

When I was satisfied with the composition, I began to think about color. I wanted to make sure the image was colorful and bold with plenty of contrast to the white of the church to make it really stand out.

SACRÉ-COEUR

When the image was complete, I began to work on the type. After choosing what would go well with the illustration, I drew two parallel lines and used them as a guide to sketch each letter freehand. Finally, I used a brush pen and fine line pen to ink up the letters on a separate sheet of paper using a lightbox. Can you spot the cat I added on every spread?

Paris remains my favorite city to visit and I hope this book inspires you to travel there.

Paul Thurlby